DINOSAUR HUNT!

A TRUE ADVENTURE

By
Rolf E. Johnson
and
Carol Ann Piggins

Library of Congress Cataloging-in-Publication Data

Johnson, Rolf E., 1956-
  Dinosaur hunt! / by Rolf E. Johnson and Carol Ann Piggins.
     p. cm. — (True adventures)
  Includes index.
  Summary: Follows members of a team of paleontologists as they
search for dinosaur remains in the Hell Creek badlands of Montana
and discover the largest fossil skull ever found.
    ISBN 0-8368-0740-5
    1. Paleontology—Juvenile literature.   [1. Paleontology.
2. Dinosaurs.]   I. Piggins, Carol Ann. II. Title. III. Series.
QE714.5.J64   1992
560—dc20   91-50336

Edited, designed, and produced by
Gareth Stevens Publishing
1555 North RiverCenter Drive, Suite 201
Milwaukee, Wisconsin 53212, USA

Series editor: Valerie Weber
Designer: Kristi Ludwig

Printed in the United States of America

2 3 4 5 6 7 8 9 98 97 96 95 94 93

For a free color catalog describing Gareth Stevens' list of high-quality
books, call 1-800-341-3569 (USA) or 1-800-461-9120 (Canada).

All pictures courtesy of the Milwaukee Public Museum, Milwaukee,
Wisconsin, except for cover and pages 6 and 10-13, all by Joseph Vance.

Editor's Note: You can find the meaning of the words in **bold** in
the glossary on page 31.

DINOSAUR HUNT!

By
Rolf E. Johnson
and
Carol Ann Piggins

Our museum decided it needed a dinosaur — a big dinosaur! A new Geology Hall was being built, and it would be the perfect home for a dinosaur skeleton. A team of **paleontologists** was put together to do the job. I was one of the paleontologists who would go on the **expedition** to find the fossil remains of a dinosaur.

Upper left: The author, Rolf Johnson, looks at other museums' dinosaur skeletons to get ideas about the kind of dinosaur the team might want for their exhibit hall.

Far left: Carpenters work with designers to get the Geology Hall ready at the Milwaukee Public Museum, home of the new dinosaur exhibit.

Canada

Hell Creek •

MONTANA

United States of America

Pacific Ocean

Hell

Creek

Formation

Fort
Peck
Reservoir

Mexico

We decided to travel to the famous Hell Creek **badlands** of northeastern Montana to begin our search. Skeletons of animals like Tyrannosaurus rex and Triceratops had been found there by other museums, so we thought that we might find a good skeleton, too. With a crew of volunteers, we set off in July to set up our base camp on the shore of the Fort Peck **Reservoir**. Would we find the dinosaur we needed?

Far left: The Hell Creek badlands are in the northeastern part of Montana.

Inset: Our expedition took place in this area.

Upper left: It takes a lot of planning and equipment for a one-month stay in the badlands. We loaded our trucks with the gear and supplies that we would need.

Left: Tents would be "home" for our expedition.

The Hell Creek badlands are famous for being rich with dinosaur fossils, but finding fossils isn't always easy. The badlands cover a lot of territory. That's why we had volunteers along to help us find the fossil bones that we were looking for.

The badlands are made up of sandstones, siltstones, and mudstones formed between 66 and 70 million years ago. In **geology,** this time span is part of the late **Cretaceous period.** Today, the badlands are slowly being worn away, or **eroding.**

Far left inset: Othniel Marsh (back row, center), a wealthy dinosaur fan, paid for many expeditions to search for dinosaur fossils in the late 1800s.

Right inset: Our expedition differed from the early ones in at least one respect — no guns!

Background: Badlands are formed when water erodes the **sedimentary** rock into **buttes,** steep hills, and deep **gullies.**

This area didn't always look hot and dry like it does today. During the late Cretaceous period, the landscape was very different. The climate was warm and moist. Lush plants covered much of the landscape, and large rivers flowed to a great inland sea in the middle of the North American continent. Dinosaurs ruled the land.

Hell Creek probably looked like this during the late Cretaceous period. Animals such as Tyrannosaurus, Ankylosaurus, Struthiomimus, and Edmontosaurus were living in Hell Creek and in what is now the North American West.

One of the most common Hell Creek dinosaurs was Triceratops, so we knew that we had a good chance of finding a Triceratops skeleton. It was one of the last members of a large family of horned dinosaurs called **ceratopsians.**

Ceratopsian dinosaurs all evolved and lived during the late Cretaceous period. They were herbivores, or plant eaters. Ceratopsian dinosaurs probably lived and traveled in large herds and used their sharp horns to defend their territory. They also used these horns to fight for their social rank in the herd.

A herd of Triceratops forms a circle, horns pointing out, to defend itself.

If you are going to hunt for dinosaur fossils, you must know where to look. You can find these fossils on every continent. But the rocks you're searching among have to be sedimentary rocks from the **Mesozoic era.**

Wherever you walk in the badlands, a fossil may lie just inches beneath your feet. But unless the rocks are actively eroding, so that fossils can be exposed at the surface, you'd never know they were there.

Fossils erode over time, too. So if you get there a few years too late, they could be gone — just bits at the bottom of a hill!

Far left: There is no other feeling like finding your first dinosaur fossil!

Left: It can take days to find even the smallest fossil fragment. We needed sharp eyes and patience.

Bob and Gail Chambers, two of our volunteers, were climbing a hill early one morning to explore a new prospecting spot. Suddenly, they stopped in their tracks. They had heard the warning sound of a rattlesnake's rattle. They knew better than to continue along that path.

Bob and Gail carefully retraced their steps. Safely out of the rattlesnake's path, they found another way up the hill they had been climbing.

Imagine their surprise when they happened upon a jumble of dinosaur bones eroding out of the rock on the hilltop!

Dangerous paths require sure footing.

Inset: Bob and Gail Chambers beam about their discovery.

Once we knew we had found a dinosaur skeleton, we could start **excavating.** First, we had to carefully remove and bag the hundreds of bone fragments scattered over the surface of the hill. Next, we painstakingly removed the sediment, exposing the rest of the bones to the first light they had "seen" in over 65 million years! Some work could be done with shovels and pick-axes; some had to be done with small dental picks and brushes.

It would take over three weeks to finish our work. Early on, we knew we had found a ceratopsian dinosaur. Was it Triceratops or the much rarer Torosaurus?

Far left: Volunteer crews, with staff supervision, take turns at the site, excavating a few bones a day.

Left: The author carefully paints a dinosaur bone with a preservative.

Work in the badlands is exciting, but it can also be hot and dirty. We have to wake up early in the morning so that we can get out into the field before the sun gets too high in the sky. Plus, the winds can be fierce. Because it's so hot and dry, we have to keep drinking lots of water.

Sometimes it rains, and then all our work comes to a stop. The hard, dry earth turns to "gumbo," a slippery, sticky mud that clings to our boots and makes it almost impossible to walk. Puddles form on the dirt roads, and cliff-side passageways can become slick and dangerous.

Far left inset: Even though we had a dinosaur skeleton to excavate, volunteers still spent each day searching the badlands for new discoveries.

Right inset: Nothing feels better than a dip in the cool Fort Peck Reservoir after a hot day's work.

Background: Digging fossils starts on our knees.

21

Each day, Dr. Robert West, our expedition leader, sent a crew to the excavation site. And each day, a few more bones were uncovered. Bones were lying on top of each other, all mixed up. It looked as though someone had taken the entire skeleton and thrown it up in the air so that the bones came down in a jumble. It would take a lot of work to put this puzzle back together again!

While we excavated the dinosaur skeleton, other volunteers kept up the search for more fossils. Each day, bones from different dinosaurs were found, excavated, and brought back to our busy base camp.

Far left: Pieces of our dinosaur puzzle mingle with our tools.

Left: Whenever we remove each fragile bone from the ground, we must wrap it in a protective plaster cast called a **field jacket**.

The day finally arrived when the bones, wrapped in protective field jackets, were ready to be taken from the hilltop. This is often a tricky business, since the bones are heavy and fragile. Dr. West made sure that we were careful not to damage our treasure.

One by one, with ropes and lots of people power, the fossils left what had been their resting place for millions of years. They were on their way to the museum.

Above: Ancient bones and relatively new bones are stacked in front of our dinosaur diggers.

Left: The museum's trucks are loaded with field jackets, each of which contains part of our dinosaur skeleton.

Back at the museum, we had a lot of work to do. We had to unpack the bones and clean them. We had to glue the many small pieces back together, and we had to study them so we could figure out how to put the skeleton together.

We **reconstructed** our dinosaur skeleton and found out that we had actually discovered a Torosaurus. What's more, it had the largest skull of any dinosaur ever found!

We have found the answers to lots of our questions. But we still have so much to learn and many badlands to explore. Who knows what great discovery lies over the next hill?

It took a lot of work to reconstruct the Torosaurus skeleton. The skull alone was nine feet (2.75 m) long and eight feet (2.5 m) wide!

We're Not Know-It-Alls . . . Yet!

It's true, we still have a lot to learn about dinosaurs and other animals that roamed the prehistoric world. But the discovery and reconstruction of our Torosaurus skeleton gave us the answers to some questions scientists have had for a long time about dinosaurs.

For example, because we were the first to find Torosaurus bones (people had only found separate skulls until our discovery), we discovered that Torosaurus did have a body that was a lot like the body of its cousin Triceratops. Also, because we uncovered the bones to a front leg, we discovered that Torosaurus and its relatives held their front legs in a reptile-like stance with bent elbows, instead of straight underneath their bodies like mammals. And because we found a healed puncture wound on the skull of our Torosaurus caused by another Torosaurus, we figured out that Torosaurs used their horns in combat with each other.

But we still have other questions:

• Why are Torosaurus fossils so rare? Hundreds of Triceratops skeletons have been found, but only six Torosaurus skulls and one Torosaurus skeleton have been found so far.

• Is Torosaurus really a separate kind of ceratopsian dinosaur or just another kind of Triceratops?

• Could the Torosaurus run or gallop? Or could it only move slowly?

• Why did the Torosaurus and all the other dinosaurs become extinct?

Every time we find the answer to one scientific question, more questions pop up. No matter how much we find out, there is always more to learn.

But There Are Some Things We Do Know . . .

Museums rarely find all of the bones from a single dinosaur skeleton. They must often reconstruct complete skeletons of dinosaurs by using both real fossil bones and copies or casts of any missing bones. The finished "composite" skeleton helps us understand what the animal's complete skeleton would look like if all of the bones had been preserved.

Just as paleontologists can piece together an incomplete skeleton and form a "composite" of a full skeleton, they piece together many bits of information that often fit together, like a puzzle, to give a picture of a dinosaur. Below are some of the puzzle pieces that scientists are putting together to form a picture of Torosaurus — known as the "Bull Lizard."

Torosaurus Trivia

• Torosaurus ate plants; it was an herbivorous dinosaur.

• Torosaurus had large, parrotlike beaks with sharp and curved cutting edges for slicing off pieces of plants.

• Torosaurus teeth acted like pinking shears to chop up the tough plants before they were swallowed.

• Torosaurus lived in North America between 66 million and 75 million years ago, during the late Cretaceous period.

• Torosaurus was an ornithischian (bird-hipped) dinosaur. This means that the front part of its hip bones pointed down and back, and its legs were held straight down from its hips, not bowed out.

• When full grown, a Torosaurus weighed between 10,000 and 14,000 pounds (4,500-6,300 kg) and was about 25 to 30 feet (7.5-9 m) long. That's bigger than a bull elephant!

• Torosaurus was among the last of the dinosaurs to roam the earth.

Organizations

The organizations listed below have more information about dinosaurs and fossils. When you write to them, tell them exactly what you need to know, and give them your full name, address, and age. Or you can contact your local university or museum.

American Museum of Natural History
Central Park West at 79th Street
New York, NY 10024

Denver Museum of Natural History
City Park
Denver, CO 80205

Dinosaur National Monument
P.O. Box 128
Jensen, UT 84035

Milwaukee Public Museum
800 West Wells Street
Milwaukee, WI 53233

National Museum of Natural History
Smithsonian Institution
Washington, DC 20560

Tyrrell Museum of Paleontology
P.O. Box 7500
Drumheller, Alberta T0J 0Y0

More Books About Dinosaurs

These books will help you discover more about dinosaurs, their fossils, and paleontology. Check with your library or bookstore to see if they have them or can order them for you.

The Big Beast Book: Dinosaurs and How They Got That Way. Booth (Little, Brown & Company)

Digging Dinosaurs. Horner and Gorman (Workman Publishing)

Dinosaur Bones. Aliki (Harper & Row)

Illustrated Encyclopedia of Dinosaurs. Norman (Crescent Books)

Maia: A Dinosaur Grows Up. Horner and Gorman (Museum of the Rockies)

Glossary

badlands — a region with very little plant life, where erosion has cut the land into a maze of deep, narrow ravines and sharp crests and pinnacles.

butte — a hill that rises sharply from the surrounding area and has sloping sides and a flat top.

Ceratopsians — horned dinosaurs that lived between 65 and 75 million years ago during the late Cretaceous period.

Cretaceous period — a period of time between 65 and 145 million years ago.

erode — to wear away. During *erosion*, earthy or rocky material is loosened or dissolved and moved on the earth's surface.

excavate — to dig out.

expedition — an organized group of people searching for something.

field jacket — a covering usually made of plaster and burlap that is used to wrap fossils. It protects them for a safe trip from the field to the museum.

geology — the science that explores the physical aspects of the earth, the rocks it's made from, and the changes on its surface.

gully — a deep ditch or channel cut in the earth by running water.

Mesozoic era — one of the large divisions of geologic time. It came after the Paleozoic era and before the Cenozoic era. Made up of the Triassic, Jurassic, and Cretaceous periods and spanning the time from 65 to 250 million years ago, this era is often called the Age of Dinosaurs.

paleontologists — scientists who explore prehistoric life, usually by studying the fossils of plants and animals.

reconstruct — to put together an animal's bones, or casts of bones.

reservoir — a place where water is held back or collected.

sedimentary rocks — rocks formed by the buildup of sediment like sand, mud, or silt, from water or air. Most fossils are found preserved in sedimentary rock.

Index

Ankylosaurus 11

badlands 7-11, 15, 21, 27

ceratopsians 13, 19, 28
climate 11, 21
Cretaceous period 9, 11, 13, 29

Edmontosaurus 11
elephant 29
equipment 7, 19, 23
erosion 9, 15, 17
excavation 19, 21, 23
extinction 28

field jackets 23, 25
Fort Peck Reservoir 7, 21
fossils 9, 15, 17, 21, 23-25, 28, 29

geology 9
Geology Hall 5
gumbo 21

Hell Creek 7-11, 13

lodging 7

Marsh, Othniel 9

Mesozoic era 15
Milwaukee Public Museum 5
Montana 7
mudstones 9
museums 5, 7, 27, 29

North America 11, 29

ornithischians 29

paleontologists 5, 29

rattlesnakes 17
reconstruction 27, 29

sandstones 9
sedimentary rocks 9, 15
siltstones 9
skeletons 5, 7, 13, 17-19, 21, 23-27, 28, 29
Struthiomimus 11

Torosaurus 19, 27, 28-29
Triceratops 7, 13, 19, 28
Tyrannosaurus rex 7, 11

volunteers 7, 17, 19, 21, 23, 25